LOW-COST GARDENING

The Gardener's Collection

Better Homes and Gardens® Books

Des Moines

BETTER HOMES AND GARDENS® BOOKS
An Imprint of Meredith® Books

LOW-COST GARDENING
Senior Editor: Marsha Jahns
Production Manager: Douglas Johnston

Vice President and Editorial Director: Elizabeth P. Rice
Executive Editor: Kay Sanders
Managing Editor: Christopher Cavanaugh
Art Director: Ernest Shelton

President, Book Group: Joseph J. Ward
Vice President, Retail Marketing: Jamie L. Martin
Vice President, Direct Marketing: Timothy Jarrell

MEREDITH CORPORATION
Chairman of the Executive Committee: E. T. Meredith III
Chairman of the Board and Chief Executive Officer: Jack D. Rehm
President and Chief Operating Officer: William T. Kerr

All of us at Meredith® Books are dedicated to providing you with the information and ideas you need to garden successfully. We guarantee your satisfaction with this book for as long as you own it. If you have any questions, comments, or suggestions, please write to us at:

MEREDITH® BOOKS, Garden Books
Editorial Department, RW 240
1716 Locust St.
Des Moines, IA 50309-3023

Produced for Meredith Corporation by Storey Communications, Inc., Schoolhouse Road, Pownal, VT 05261
Editor: Gwen W. Steege
Production: Laurie Musick Wright
Writer: Pat Nichols
Photographers: PHOTO/NATS: Gay Bumgarner, cover, pages 13, 27 (thyme), 41, 54–55, 63; David Cavagnaro, pages 3, 45, 57, 59; Priscilla Connell, page 35; Wally Eberhart, pages 29 (broccoli), 46–47; Jennifer Graylock, pages 32–33; Bill Larkin, page 43; Robert E. Lyons, pages 23 (aster), 37, 39; Julie O'Neil, pages 11, 14–15; Jennie Plumley, page 9; Laura C. Scheibel, pages 6–7, 61; Virginia Twinam-Smith, page 53; Marilyn Wood, pages 17, 18, 19, 31. Also, All-America Selections, pages 23 (pansy), 27 (lavender), 29 (beans).
Illustrator: Brigita Fuhrmann

Growing beautiful flowers and luscious vegetables rewards the gardener with the pleasure of accomplishment. Doing so for the least amount of money adds satisfaction.

CONTENTS

Setting Your Goals 6

Growing from Seed 14

Penny-Pinching Tips 32

Getting the Most from Your Tools 46

Gardening for Your Home 54

Index 64

Setting Your Goals

*P*lan a high-impact, small-scale garden. In the long run, a good solid plan keeps expenses to a minimum. Think about what you hope to accomplish and which plants you like to grow. Consider the total look, especially for flower gardens. Select the best place for your garden. And if you're just beginning, keep your garden small!

Your Garden Plan

Make a "map" of your garden on graph paper before you dig into the soil. Use colored construction paper to represent groups of flowers. Move them around to assess the visual impact of the flower garden you picture. Do the same for vegetables. Estimate the amount of vegetables your family uses.

Enlarge or reduce the size of the cutouts as your plan evolves. This master plan will save time and money whether your interest lies in flowers or vegetables or both.

Work on the plan, set it aside, and reconsider until you feel each element works in a complementary way. Strive for a total effect. Remember it's much easier to move colored paper than to dig up actual plants once they are in the ground. And you'll save money by buying only what you need.

Gardener's Tip

Some gardeners like sharply defined rows, straight as an arrow; others prefer a softer look. You make the choice.

Consider the amount of sun or shade your planned-for garden receives. Try to avoid planting under or near large trees, which cast shade and also rob your garden of water and nutrients.

Take into account your own likes and dislikes. Does a casual country look appeal to you? Have you always yearned for a more formal garden? Whatever your choice, keep it in mind as you decide what flowers or vegetables to plant.

Mark on your layout where you will expand your garden in the future, so that you spread the costs over several years.

Think small at first. Match your garden size to the amount of time and money you can devote to it. The smaller the plot, the less of everything you need. A 5-x-10-foot garden takes half as many plants as a 10-x-20-foot garden. A small garden takes less fertilizer, less mulch, less water, fewer seeds, fewer stakes, and less work.

Make a budget, set priorities, and establish realistic goals about what you plan to spend the first year.

A small garden with a big impact glows with red, pink, and white zinnias, combined with purple salvia.

Start a record book. Keep track of costs. Once you see how your budget works, you gain a better idea about what expenses to expect in years to come. When you estimate future expenditures, review your actual expenses and look for ways to cut costs.

List projects in order of priority, knowing you can move or change the order. Set aside money for new plants or plants to replace those that did not prosper.

Make long-term allotments for the expenses of seeds, plants, tools, and other needs. Make a three- or five-year plan for additional acquisitions. Start small and simple with a minimum number of plants and only essential tools the first year.

Gardener's Tip

Place your garden in a spot where you can expand it in the future, if you desire.

Getting into the Garden

Don't buy more plants than you need. Consider the mature height and breadth of your plants when you put in young seedings. Like children, they grow quickly and you may be forced to move or dispose of plants that become crowded. Better to add more plants next year, than to overplant in your enthusiasm.

Start with easy-to-maintain plants, ones you know or like, or those recommended for their suitability. Add to your collection each year as finances allow.

Jot down especially successful plants that grow well. Note where you buy the plants, how many you buy, and how much they cost. Also include information on the plants that don't work — and why.

Gardener's Tip

Look for specials on film and developing costs. Take advantage of second-print-free offers.

Compare costs and results. Plants that don't suit your garden are a waste of money.

Use your camera to photograph plants that could fit in your garden. When you visit other gardens, snap photos of sections that appeal to you, then incorporate the ideas in your own planning. Note the orientation of the sun, and whether there is partial sun or shade. On the back of the prints, write all the information you have collected and use the photos for reference.

Chronicle your own garden by photographing it as it changes over the gardening season. Use this record to visualize what changes would be effective or note where the garden needs some additional plants or extra attention. Take photos from a distance, including the whole garden or flower bed, then come in close for specific plants.

Start with easy-to-maintain annuals like dianthus, marigolds, and zinnias.

Cut from the Top

Small savings are always beneficial, but you'll get the most impact when you tackle the high-cost items. Here are some suggestions for how to cut costly items or cut them out of your budget.

■ Spread costs over time. If you want a watering system or a fence, consider installing in segments. Start this year with a section or two, add several more the next year, and so on. Eventually it adds up to a complete installation, but costs spread out over time are easier to absorb.

■ Do it yourself. Instead of a fully assembled garden cart, you may be able to purchase a kit or find plans to build one from scratch.

■ Get together. Co-purchase equipment with a friend and split the cost. Some big items are necessary only occasionally, and sharing makes sense.

■ Look for low-cost tilling ads. You may find that local service organizations, Boy Scouts, for instance, do rototilling reasonably during spring months.

■ Buy second-hand equipment. If you are a vegetable gardener, buy a second-hand rototiller. Place your own advertisement for one. Classifieds in daily newspapers offer reasonable prices, or use the free shoppers found in super-markets where ads cost only a couple of dollars. Put an ad on a bulletin board.

■ Plant perennials. They will come back year after year, whereas annuals grow, bloom, and die in one year. With perennials, you don't have to replant each year, so you save money.

■ Buy seed instead of plants, whether you grow annuals or perennials. Some perennials started this way may not bloom until the second year, but the savings make the wait worthwhile.

■ Buy plants from nonprofit groups, such as conservation organizations, that sell berry plants, trees, flower bulbs, even asparagus plants at very reasonable prices as fund-raisers. They may insist on preordering. Plants arrive at the proper planting time for your region.

■ Buy smaller one-year-old perennials instead of more mature (and more expensive) ones. Plant in a nursery row for a year or two. Once they are permanently settled in, they reach the same dimensions for less money. In addition, they acclimate to the individual growing conditions of your garden.

■ Wait to purchase unusual, rare, or new plants until they have been on the market a few seasons. At first they cost more than common varieties; later, prices drop.

■ Buy fertilizers, peat moss, lime, seed-starting equipment, and other garden supplies on sale. Garden centers and hardware stores run

Install a picket fence in sections, to spread costs over time. Stained, for a natural look, this section makes a good setting for bright zinnias.

specials on garden supplies regularly.

■ Make your own compost. Look for sources of free manure and mulch materials.

■ Use your imagination to make your garden interesting. Improvise garden containers from old buckets or boxes. Look for statuary seconds. Scout tag or estate sales for good buys on garden furniture instead of buying new.

Growing from Seed

Starting plants from seed not only saves money, it also ensures total control over the varieties and numbers you plant. You oversee the whole process. As the tiny plants emerge, you choose the strongest to nurture.

Save on Seed

When you start your own plants from seed, you expand your choices to a larger number of varieties, each with different qualities. Some offer better disease resistance, others a larger palette of colors. Some grow better in a specific region than others. You also can try unusual varieties that may be difficult to find from commercial growers, who tend to grow the more well-known plants.

Try several different varieties of each flower or vegetable to find the ones that best serve your needs. When you start your own, you know your plants more intimately, what light suits them, how often to feed them, and eventually how well they bloom and yield.

Plan to buy on sale if possible. Garden-seed costs mount quickly, but many stores run half-price end-of-season sales. You won't find as much choice, but the savings are substantial — often up to 50 percent off seed from well-known

> ## Gardener's Tip
> To test the vitality of leftover seed, place a few on a wet paper towel and keep them moist. If the seeds sprout after the proper time, go ahead and plant them. If you get less than 50 percent germination, buy new.

companies. Most seeds stay viable for years.

Study the seed packet or catalog, and note disease resistance, length of time to maturity, and mature size. Keep in mind that each region of the country, and every garden, has different growing conditions. Whether you grow flowers or vegetables, unsuitable plants cost the gardener loss of time and productivity. It doesn't matter how beautiful plants look in a catalog: If they require more sun, less water, a different kind of soil, or cooler temperatures than you can provide, they will fail to grow well. Failures are a disappointment and a loss to your gardening dollar.

Make your own potting soil. Try this mixture: Combine two parts soil, one part sand, perlite, or vermiculite, and one part compost (see pages 38–39). Add 1 tablespoon of bonemeal. Sterilize this mixture by placing it on a tray in a regular oven set at 150°F for 30 minutes, or in a plastic bag (punch a few holes in it) in a microwave oven for four or five minutes.

Starting plants from seed is one of the best ways to save costs in flower and vegetable gardens alike.

Starting Seed Indoors

Starting seed indoors is fun, a breath of spring when the cold still hangs on outside. Here's how to do it.

Collect plastic and cardboard containers to use as seed-starting trays. Recycled supermarket produce trays, milk cartons, or other shallow containers work well. Find additional ideas for seed-starting trays on page 42.

Sprinkle seed on moistened soil mix.

Purchase seed-starting soil or make some, using the recipe on page 17.

Select seed for plants that need a long growing season, such as tomatoes and peppers, or favorite flowers that you want to grow in large quantities or in very specific colors.

Calculate the length of time between seed sowing and the safe time to plant your seedlings in the garden. Don't start seed too early. They will become spindly or fail to thrive. Check the seed packet for advice on when to plant indoors.

Fill seed-starting containers almost to the top with potting mix. Moisten the mixture well. Make shallow furrows, plant the seeds at the depth indicated on the seed packet, and cover lightly with more soil.

Gardener's Tip

If you find handling very small seeds frustrating, put them in an old salt shaker with a small amount of sand and sprinkle them on the soil mix.

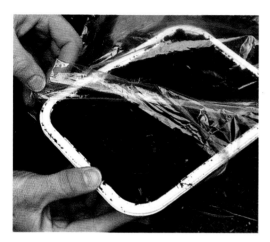

Slip the seed tray into a plastic bag to maintain moisture level.

Remove plastic after seeds sprout.

Mark planting containers with a waterproof marking pencil. When seedlings first emerge, they all look alike to the novice.

Gently water soil mix again, taking care not to disturb the seeds. Place containers in plastic bags to maintain humidity and close with a twist-tie or tuck under the tray.

Place seed trays near a radiator or other heating element, or on an old electric blanket covered with plastic. Seeds need a warm place to germinate.

Watch carefully for signs of sprouting. Germination times vary from a few days to a few weeks; refer to the seed packet for guidance.

Once seedlings emerge, remove the plastic covering and place plants under lights or in a sunny location.

Gardener's Tip

To avoid damping-off disease, use sterilized soil and provide space for air to circulate between seedlings.

Seedling Care

Provide seedlings with about 12 hours of light a day. The best way to provide this much light indoors is to put your plants under fluorescent lights. Consider building a simple plant-growing unit with adjustable shelves and fluorescent lights. Make the unit freestanding, or put up shelves in a spare closet.

Keep lights close to plants just after sowing. This will keep the plants from becoming leggy (overtall with long, weak stems). As the seedlings grow, move the lights away to encourage growth.

Transplant to larger pots. When the second set of leaves emerges, seedlings should be transplanted into individual pots. By transplanting seedlings to bigger pots, you help them establish better root systems.

Prepare these pots by filling them with soil mix and watering well ahead of time. Pop each plant out of the original seed flat with a plastic knife or popsicle stick.

Gardener's Tip

Special grow lights cost more money than fluorescent ones, yet recent research indicates plants grow well under either. Save even more by finding fluorescent fixtures on sale.

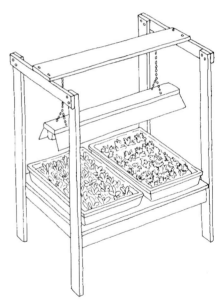

A simple setup for starting seeds indoors consists of a shelf with a fluorescent shop light suspended overhead. Adjust the height of the light so that it hangs about 6 inches above the plants.

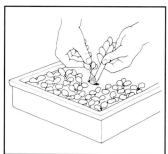

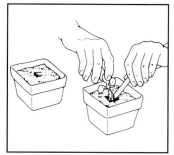

Seedlings are fragile: water them gently with a sprinkler or plant mister.

When plant trays become crowded, lift seedlings out and replant them in larger pots.

Handling a seedling by a leaf rather than by the stem, lower it into a hole in the new pot and firm the soil around it.

Poke a hole in the soil in the larger pot, place the seedling gently in the hole, then press the soil around it.

Check the plants at least once a day. Water gently with room-temperature water. Don't overwater. Look for insect pests or evidence of other problems, such as damping off (a disease that causes plants to rot at the soil line).

Apply liquid fertilizer at half strength every week or so.

Two or three weeks before you plan to place plants in the garden, start putting them outside for short periods of time each day to accustom them to the outdoors. Never set plants out on a windy day without protection or leave them in the sun until they grow quite sturdy. Increase time spent outdoors slowly until plants thoroughly acclimatize.

10 Low-Cost Annuals

1. ASTER
Callistephus chinensis
Conditions: Full sun; average soil
Color: White, purple, blue, pink, rose
Height: 6–30 inches
Comments: Good cut flowers; stake tall varieties

2. CALENDULA
Calendula officinalis
Conditions: Full sun or part shade; average soil
Color: Yellow, orange
Height: 1–2 feet
Comments: For continuous bloom, remove faded flowers; edible petals

3. COSMOS
Cosmos species
Conditions: Full sun or part shade; light average soil
Color: White, pink, lavender, orange, red
Height: 1–8 feet
Comments: Feathery foliage; good cut flowers; stake tall varieties

4. IMPATIENS
Impatiens wallerana
Conditions: Moist shade
Color: Red, orange, pink, violet, white
Height: 8–14 inches
Comments: Low maintenance; blooms all summer

5. MARIGOLD
Tagetes species
Conditions: Full sun; average soil
Color: Yellow, orange, cream,
Height: 1–3 feet
Comments: Good cut flowers; bloom from midsummer to frost

6. MORNING GLORY
Ipomoea species
Conditions: Full sun; average soil
Color: Blue, purple, pink, rose
Height: To 10 feet
Comments: Soak and nick seeds before planting; vine makes good screen

7. NASTURTIUM
Tropaeolum species
Conditions: Full sun; not too rich or too moist soil
Color: Red, orange, yellow
Height: 1–4 feet
Comments: Some double flowers; good for baskets; edible flowers

8. PANSY

Viola species

Conditions: Full sun; rich soil

Color: Purple, blue, pink, yellow, orange combinations

Height: 6–12 inches

Comments: Good for edgings and containers

9. SWEET PEA

Lathyrus odoratus

Conditions: Tolerates some shade; average soil

Color: Blue, purple, pink, white

Height: To 6 feet

Comments: Soak seeds before sowing; provide support; keep blooms cut

10. ZINNIA

Zinnia species

Conditions: Full sun; fertile soil

Color: Red, pink, purple, orange, yellow, white, green

Height: 10–36 inches

Comments: For continuous bloom, remove faded flowers; blossoms 2–6 inches across

1. Aster

2. Calendula

3. Cosmos

4. Impatiens

5. Marigold

6. Morning Glory

7. Nasturtium

8. Pansy

9. Sweet Pea

10. Zinnia

10 Low-Cost Perennials

1. BABY'S–BREATH
Gypsophila species

Conditions: Full sun; well-drained neutral soil
Color: White, pale pink, pink
Height: 4–36 inches
Comments: Stake tall varieties; use fresh or dried

2. BLEEDING-HEART
Dicentra species

Conditions: Sun or partial shade; moist, well-drained soil
Color: Pink, rose, white
Height: 10–24 inches
Comments: Heart-shaped flowers; blooms in early spring; divide in early fall

3. CANDYTUFT
Iberis species

Conditions: Full sun; average soil
Color: White, violet, pink
Height: To 16 inches
Comments: Blooms in spring; use as edging or in rock gardens

4. CANTERBURY BELLS
Campanula species

Conditions: Full sun
Color: Blue, lavender, pink, white
Height: 2–4 feet
Comments: Provide space to encourage bloom; best in informal gardens

5. COREOPSIS
Coreopsis species

Conditions: Full sun; moist soil
Color: Bright yellow, orange, red
Height: To 2 feet
Comments: For continuous bloom, remove faded flowers; single and semi-double blossoms

6. DAISY (SHASTA)
Chrysanthemum maximum

Conditions: Avoid wet areas; provide winter protection
Color: White with yellow center
Height: 2–3 feet
Comments: Single, double, and fringed forms; keep faded flowers picked

7. DELPHINIUM
Delphinium species

Conditions: Full sun; rich alkaline soil
Color: Blue, purple, lilac, pink, white
Height: 3–6 feet

Comments: Hardy, vigorous, easy to start from seed; stake tall varieties

8. FORGET-ME-NOT
Myosotis species

Conditions: Damp soil
Color: Blue flowers with gold centers
Height: 4–15 inches
Comments: Freely self-sows

9. FOXGLOVE
Digitalis species

Conditions: Sun or light shade; avoid wet soils in winter

Color: Red, yellow, purple, white
Height: To 4 feet
Comments: Showy, bell-like flowers

10. YARROW
Achillea species

Conditions: Full sun; tolerates poor soil
Color: Pink, yellow, white
Height: 18–36 inches
Comments: Blooms throughout summer; good dried

1. Baby's–Breath

2. Bleeding-Heart

3. Candytuft

4. Canterbury Bells

5. Coreopsis

6. Daisy

7. Delphinium

8. Forget-Me-Not

9. Foxglove

10. Yarrow

10 Low-Cost Herbs

1. BASIL
Ocimum basilicum
Type: Annual
Conditions: Full sun; rich soil
Comments: Pinch flower buds to increase bushiness
Uses: With tomatoes, eggs, meats

2. CHIVES
Allium schoenoprasum
Type: Perennial
Conditions: Full sun; sandy, well-drained soil
Comments: Divide clumps
Uses: Leaves in salads; lavender blossom in dried arrangements

3. CORIANDER
Coriandrum sativum
Type: Annual
Conditions: Full sun or partial shade; moderately rich, well-drained soil
Comments: Sow seed in early spring; do not transplant
Uses: Leaves in salsa; seeds in curries

4. LAVENDER
Lavandula angustifolia
Type: Perennial
Conditions: Full sun; light soil
Comments: Mulch over winter
Uses: Flowers in baking, dried arrangements, and sachets

5. LEMON BALM
Melissa officinalis
Type: Perennial
Conditions: Poor, dry soil; full sun or partial shade
Comments: Grow by seed or division
Uses: Tea, sachets, and potpourris

6. MINT
Mentha species
Type: Perennial
Conditions: Partial shade; good, moist, well-drained soil
Comments: Provide underground barrier to control rampant spreading
Uses: In teas; with lamb

7. PARSLEY
Petroselinum crispum
Type: Biennial
Conditions: Full sun or partial shade; rich, moist soil
Comments: Soak seed before sowing

Uses: Salads, soups, meat, fish, poultry

8. SORREL
Rumex scutatus
Type: Perennial
Conditions: Full sun or partial shade; rich, moist, well-drained soil
Comments: Sharp, lemony taste
Uses: Young leaves in salads

9. TARRAGON
Artemisia dracunculus
Type: Perennial

Conditions: Full sun but tolerates some shade; well-drained soil
Comments: Purchase young plants or take cuttings or divisions;
Uses: Fish and chicken

10. THYME
Thymus species
Type: Perennial
Conditions: Full sun; light soil
Comments: Good in rock gardens
Uses: Soups, sauces, chicken, fish, meats

1. Basil   *2. Chives*   *3. Coriander*   *4. Lavender*   *5. Lemon Balm*

6. Mint   *7. Parsley*   *8. Sorrel*   *9. Tarragon*   *10. Thyme*

10 Low-Cost Vegetables

1. BEANS (BUSH AND POLE)
Phaseolus vulgaris
Conditions: Full sun
Planting: Soil temperature at least 60°F for germination; place seed 2 inches apart and 1 inch deep
Comments: Provide support for climbers; avoid harvesting when leaves are damp

2. BROCCOLI
Brassica oleracea
Conditions: Full sun; rich, deep soil
Planting: Sow seeds indoors in spring for summer crop and in midsummer for fall crop
Comments: Water and supply nitrogen fertilizer

3. CABBAGE
Brassica oleracea
Conditions: Full sun; rich, deep soil
Planting: Sow seeds indoors in spring for summer crop and in midsummer for fall crop
Comments: Use compost; water during dry spells

4. CAULIFLOWER
Brassica oleracea
Conditions: Deep, rich soil
Planting: Sow seeds indoors in early spring for spring crop and in June for fall crop
Comments: Tie leaves over developing heads to blanch head

5. CUCUMBER
Cucumis sativus
Conditions: Moderately heavy soil; keep watered
Planting: May be started indoors, 3–4 seeds to a pot; thin to 1–2 plants
Comments: Mulch around plants

6. LEEK
Allium ampeloprasum
Conditions: Full sun; very fertile, well-limed soil
Planting: Sow seed 5–6 inches deep
Comments: Keep well watered

7. LETTUCE

Lactuca sativa

Conditions: Tolerates some shade

Planting: Easy to start indoors from seed; make succession plantings outdoors

Comments: Use compost; add lime to acidic soil

8. PEPPER

Capsicum annuum

Conditions: Tolerates infertile soil; needs long, warm growing season

Planting: Begin from seed indoors

Comments: Add lime to acidic soil

9. SUMMER SQUASH

Cucurbita pepo

Conditions: Moderately heavy soil; keep watered

Planting: Sow 8–10 seed in a small circle; thin to 3–4 plants

Comments: Mulch around plants

10. TOMATO

Lycopersicon esculentum

Conditions: Warm, fertile soil

Planting: Begin from seed indoors

Comments: Use mulch or black plastic; look for disease-resistant varieties; plant early, mid-, and late-season varieties

1. Beans

2. Broccoli

3. Cabbage

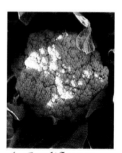

4. Cauliflower

5. Cucumber

6. Leek

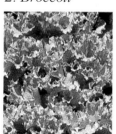

7. Lettuce

8. Pepper

9. Summer Squash

10. Tomato

Save on Plants

You may not always want, or be able, to start plants from seed. Even if you have to buy plants, however, you still can keep costs down.

■ Scout out plant sales for nonprofit organizations. Schools that have student-run greenhouses may sell high-quality plants in the spring, usually at very good prices. Other organizations, such as garden clubs and churches, also sell plants they grow. Pick up newly divided perennials, annuals, vegetable plants, and herbs at these sales, usually at very reasonable prices. At the same time, you support a good cause.

■ Some national commercial growers sell large flats of very tiny, inexpensive annuals called plugs. Impatiens are commonly offered. These can be just right for big areas that you want to fill with lots of flowers. Though the plants are quite small in the beginning, they reach a mature size quickly, and by midsummer fill in large beds nicely. Look for ads for such growers in gardening magazines, resource books, or trade magazines. Consider making up a large order with friends and neighbors who also need plants.

■ Small greenhouses run as a hobby often offer plants at lower prices than big establishments.

■ Visit farmers' markets where plants are sold. Many small growers sell good-quality, reasonably priced flats of vegetables and flowers. Most sellers offer planting and growing advice. Sometimes sellers reduce prices late in the day rather than take plants home. Selection offered is often impressive and varied.

■ After the first splurge of planting, most greenhouses cut prices on annuals. Wait a bit and then buy on sale.

Gardener's Tip

Consider starting a plant fund-raiser of your own. Ask members of an organization you support to grow and nurture a few flats of flowers or vegetables, then donate them to the sale.

■ Share costs with friends. Form a gardening club and buy or prepare potting mix together. Plant extra plants to share or trade. Buy seed in large quantities at lower cost, then divide it among an ordering group.

■ Let friends and neighbors know you need plants. Most gladly will give you the excess when they thin out borders or gardens. Stay adaptable; the colors may not suit you at the time, but the price is right. Most of the time, you end up with an abundance of plants perfect for your garden.

■ Avoid "too-good-to-be-true" bargain plants. Plants that seem too cheap may not have had a good start with strong healthy roots. Before you purchase any plants — especially those that seem underpriced — examine them closely. Turn leaves over to inspect the underside. Look for evidence of disease or insect infestation. If leaves droop or look yellowed or if a plant is leggy or weedy, you probably shouldn't buy it. Sometimes newly transplanted seedlings look good temporarily

The selection and prices at small, local nurseries or farmer's markets may be quite attractive.

but never prosper because they lack a solid root system. Check plants by giving them a gentle tug to see if they hug the soil.

Gardener's Tip

Community greenhouse groups often prepare and bag fine-quality potting soil to sell to the public.

31

Penny-Pinching Tips

*P*lants need water
and healthy soil, and
protection from harsh
conditions, nutrients,
insect pests, and
disease. Penny-
pinching gardeners
look for ways to provide
all of these as frugally
as possible.

Watering without Waste

All plants need water. The gardener must provide what does not issue from the heavens. Watering gardens can be an expensive undertaking in some situations.

Improve soil. Some soils hold water better than others. Water runs through gravelly, sandy soils; it runs off hard-packed clay soils. In both cases, water never reaches the roots of the plants. Improve any soil's ability to hold water by adding compost (see page 38).

Plant right. Some plants do well in a slight depression that traps water for slow release to the roots.

Timing helps. Water in the evening or early in the morning when the effects last longer. If you water at night, however, avoid getting water on the leaves of densely growing plants. This is especially true in humid conditions where mildew and other plant disease is a problem. Soaker hoses, which keep water in the soil and off the leaves, are good alternatives to sprinklers.

Water slowly. If you water too quickly, the soil is unable to absorb the water, which runs off wasted. Drip systems and soaker hoses not only water slowly, but they efficiently and effectively put the water where the plants need it — around their roots.

Drip systems and soaker hoses require an initial cash outlay, but in the long run they save you money, and they also conserve water for the health of the environment. Drip setups consist of a system of hoses with outlets that can be directed to specific plants. Soaker hoses, which are buried slightly under the surface of the soil throughout the garden, are made of a porous material that allows the water to slowly seep out into the soil along the entire length of the hose.

Gardener's Tip

Black plastic and other mulches conserve water by inhibiting evaporation.

Drought-resistant plants. Certain plants require much more water than others. If you live where water restrictions affect use or where water is metered, look for drought-resistant plant varieties.

Container plants. Grow plants in containers and group them together. You'll save time watering them. Set containers into the ground if possible to save water, because there's less evaporation through the sides of the pot.

Homemade systems. Develop a homemade drip system for individual in-ground plants. Poke a tiny hole in the bottom of a plastic gallon milk bottle. Fill the bottle with water and place it in the garden near a plant. These are ideal for tomato plants.

Find alternatives. Save rainwater in barrels to use on plants. Consider an inexpensive pump system if you have access to a pond or some other body of water suitable for use on the garden.

It takes less time to water container plants if you group them together. Arrange pleasing combinations like this tall annual salvia, graceful lobelia, and bright red geraniums, against yellow marigolds.

Mulches that Save

Mulch is a material you spread around plants, usually 2 or 3 inches deep, to discourage weeds and reduce the loss of water in the soil from evaporation. Mulches can be organic or nonorganic. Some good low-cost mulches include pine needles, straw, sawdust, grass clippings, black plastic, even newspapers.

Carpet scraps. Ask your local carpet dealer for leftover scraps from installations. These may be free or very low cost. Spread the pieces between rows of vegetables to keep down weeds, keep soil warm, and conserve water. Discard after a year or two.

Grass clippings make good, free mulch, as do leaves. Use them for mulch during the gardening season, then dig or plow them under in autumn to add organic matter to the soil.

Wood chips are a commonly used mulch. Commercially packaged shredded bark or bark chips look good, but costs mount if you use them over large areas. Look for a nearby saw- or lumber mill to buy quantities for less money. Or check with utility companies that constantly clear brush away near wires. They shred it into particles suitable for mulching and often offer it free to gardeners. If you plan to cut down a tree or know someone who does, rent a shredder that makes the wood usable as mulch. Always feed wood into a shredder with great care to avoid accidents. Get together with someone else who needs mulch and split the costs and work.

Gardener's Tip

Don't put grass clippings on the garden until they dry for a day or two. Clippings tend to heat up so much when they first begin to decompose that they can actually damage plant parts.

Appearance counts. Don't use a particular mulch just because it costs little or nothing. Before you decide to use it, consider how it looks. A cheap hay mulch works fine in a vegetable garden deep in the back of your property, but it won't add to the aesthetics of the flower garden you prize. Use wood chips here instead. Dark, fine coffee grounds spread around flowers can be an attractive mulch.

Some mulches contribute significantly to your soil. Seaweed is excellent mulch for those near an ocean; it adds potassium to the soil. If you use hay around vegetables, it lightens the soil.

Gardener's Tip

Be creative with mulches. Use different ones in different places. Consider mixing two kinds for a unique look.

Black plastic makes an excellent mulch for tomatoes, peppers, and eggplants. Use the lighter weight plastic. It won't last as long, but it handles easier and costs less than the heavier version. If the shine bothers you, scatter grass clippings over it.

These 'Spicy Globe' basils are neatly mulched with shredded bark.

Free Food for Your Garden

Compost—decayed organic matter similar to that on a forest floor — is the gardener's best friend. It supplies nutrients to the soil and helps the soil retain water. And, it essentially comes free!

Save scraps. Anyone can make compost. You don't need expensive composting bins or containers. To produce compost in the simplest way, find a corner of your yard where you can pile kitchen and garden waste, such as vegetable peelings and coffee grounds (no meat or animal products), grass clippings, small twigs and branches, faded blossoms from flowers, and leaves. Add some soil, peat moss, lime, and/or manure, and turn the pile with a garden fork occasionally. When your compost reaches a deep dark, crumbly state (in about four to six months),

spread it on the garden. Dig it in, or use it as a mulch around plants, then dig it in during the fall. After you see how easy composting is, you'll want to maintain three piles in various stages of development.

Construct simple compost bins using inexpensive wire mesh or wooden fencing to surround the compost material.

To hide the pile, position plantings around the area. Leave an opening to keep the compost accessible.

A properly working compost heap does not smell. Occasionally, however (for instance, if you pile too many grass clippings on at one time), you may notice a disagreeable odor. Add some lime, give it a few turns, and the odor will soon disappear.

Speed the composting process by adding some soil. Throw in weeds with the soil that adheres to their roots, and add one or two shovelfuls from the garden occasionally.

Gardener's Tip

Golf courses generate a lot of grass clippings. Ask to take some for your garden or compost pile.

Freely vining morning glories ramble over this simple wood-frame compost bin.

Fertilizers. The main ingredients in general-purpose garden fertilizers are nitrogen, phosphorus, and potassium in different ratios.

Commercial fertilizers tend to be expensive. Try to buy them on sale. Large-size bags cost less per pound, so you realize a savings if you buy in quantity. If you don't need a lot, split the bag and the costs with a gardening friend. Fertilizer keeps well for several seasons.

If you live in or near the country, farmers may let you haul away horse, cow, or chicken manure for your garden. Some may even deliver. Use only well-rotted manure on your garden.

If you burn wood, spread the ashes on the garden, then dig them in as you prepare the soil for planting. Ashes supply potassium.

State fisheries and wildlife divisions often kill fish at certain times of the year. Find out if they allow gardeners to pick up the remains to use as fertilizer. These may smell, but they are an excellent soil-improver.

Waging a Low-Cost War

Plant diseases and pests invade almost all gardens at one time or another. Controls such as sprays or powders increase gardening costs. To avoid problems, take some precautions ahead of time.

The best low-cost way to have a healthy garden is to practice garden hygiene. A clean, well-kept garden discourages bugs and diseases. Remove spent flowers and other plant refuse. Burn diseased plants. In the vegetable garden, rotate crops from one area to another each season.

Leave as much room as possible between plants and rows to allow good air circulation and fast drying after a rain. Water a little less; plants develop a tougher covering that some insects avoid.

Use disease-resistant varieties. Some varieties of plants are prone to disease. For instance, look for tomato plants bred specifically to resist fusarium and verticillium wilts.

Companion plants. Some strong-smelling plants discourage insect infestation. Onions, for instance, deter most pests; marigolds discourage tomato worms and asparagus beetles. Most insects dislike asters. Some plants seem to have characteristics that complement one another; others grow poorly when planted nearby. For example, many gardeners plant bush beans near carrots, beets, or cabbage, but away from onions; do plant onions near celery or peppers.

Many herbs make good garden neighbors. Tomatoes do well near mint, basil, and chives. Basil

Gardener's Tip

Hand-picking slugs, beetles, and tomato or cabbage worms costs nothing. Knock these and other similar creatures off the plant with a strong blast of water from a hose. Or, brush them off into a can of soapy water.

discourages flies and mosquitoes; horseradish deters the potato bug. Caraway helps loosen the soil; thyme sends the cabbage worm packing. Rue repels fleas and Japanese beetles. Both thyme and rosemary repel many insects.

It costs little to make your own sprays and pest deterrents, and these can control insects and diseases.

Soap spray: 3 tablespoons soap powder in 1 gallon water. Spray foliage; try to hit the insects directly. Use against soft-bodied insects, such as mealybugs, aphids, and spider mites.

Baking soda spray: 1 tablespoon baking soda, 1 tablespoon cooking oil, and 1 gallon of water. Spray on rose bushes about once a week to reduce mildew and blackspot.

Beer: Place shallow containers of beer in the garden to trap slugs.

Soap: Hang hotel-size bars of soap around tulips to deter deer.

"Insect juice": ½ cup insect pest (Japanese beetles, for instance) and 2 cups of water whirred in an old

A clean, orderly garden, with rows and plants well spaced to allow good air circulation, is a positive first step in avoiding garden pests and diseases.

blender (one you no longer use in the kitchen) until liquefied. Strain and used about ¼ cup to 1 gallon water. Spray entire surface of the plant.

Garlic spray: 1 head garlic and 2 cups water whirred in a blender. Dilute this concentrate with an equal amount of water and spray entire plant.

Hot pepper spray: Grind hot peppers until liquefied. Add ginger and a drop or two of soap. Spray directly on plants.

Recycled Treasure

Finding unexpected treasures among your recyclables is like money in your pocket. If you use your imagination, you can make trellises, plant protectors, plant markers, seed-starting setups, and numerous other articles from items other people throw away.

- Cut plastic containers into strips and use as labels to mark rows or identify seed trays. Use waterproof permanent markers for notations.
- Convert empty half-gallon milk cartons into pots for young tomato or pepper transplants. Cut to desired height, make several holes in the bottom for drainage, and use for larger transplants.
- Use the 2-inch-deep plastic or pressed cardboard containers from supermarket delis or produce departments as seed-starting trays. As seedlings develop, either transplant them to other containers or thin to six to eight plants per tray. Be sure to make drainage holes in the bottom.
- Neatly fold several thicknesses of newspaper to form small individual seed-starting pots.
- Use shallow cardboard boxes to hold peat pots or other small pots with young seedlings.
- Use egg cartons as individual starting pots. Other useful containers for starting seeds include yogurt and cottage cheese containers, cardboard milk and cream cartons, and plastic and Styrofoam food or beverage servers of all sizes.
- Store seeds in baby-food jars.
- Fashion a gallon or half-gallon plastic milk jug into a scoop and use to dispense garden mixtures such as fertilizer, lime, and potting soil. Label each scoop according to use; keep separate scoops for each mixture.
- Use empty 5-gallon plastic containers, such as the ones joint compound comes in, as portable storage for fertilizer or potting soil.
- Visit garage sales for buys on used pots, watering cans (mend leaks with silicon caulking), wheelbarrows, arches, and garden furniture. Goodwill Industries or Salvation Army secondhand stores

are other good sources of equipment.

■ Wear old elbow-length gloves when you work around prickly plants like roses, squash, and brambles.

■ Slip a foam rubber pad (or use an old pillow) into a plastic bag and use as a kneeling pad when working in the garden, especially in slightly wet conditions. This is a good use of extra shopping bags.

■ Keep an old mailbox (or other waterproof container) near the garden to hold odds and ends like string, gloves, or markers. Brighten the mailbox with new paint.

■ Use industrial packing pallets to keep the compost heap slightly elevated for air circulation. Many businesses will give these away. If you find any good wood in them, recycle it into small building projects — new planters, for instance.

■ Turn an old door into a potting table. Lay it across sawhorses, and keep supplies and pots below.

■ Reuse string in the garden to mark rows, aid climbing vines,

This old rowboat may no longer be seaworthy, but it makes a whimsical raised bed for pansies and annual dwarf chrysanthemums.

make trellises for beans and peas, and keep plants from flopping over.

■ Recycle your Christmas tree. Make it the center pole of a tepee by running five or six lengths of string from the top to the ground, securing the string with stakes, and planting pole beans at the base.

More Recycled Treasure

■ Erect 12- to 18-inch-long branches (shrub prunings are perfect) among young perennials that need staking. The flowers will be supported invisibly by the branches as they grow.

■ Stack old screens with blocks of wood as spacers to dry onions, shallots, garlic, herbs, and dried flowers before storage.

■ Newspapers make good mulch, but don't stop there. Cut wide bands to put around the base of new transplants to discourage cutworms.

■ Cut the bottoms off plastic gallon milk jugs and settle them over transplants in the garden to protect from spring frosts.

■ Protect young plants under an inexpensive cloche made with a wire coat-hanger frame. Bend two hangers into U shapes and place one on each side of the plant, pushing the wire ends firmly into the soil. Cover the frame with gardening cloth or plastic. Anchor the cover at the corners with rocks.

■ Prop two old window screens against one another to make an A-frame windbreak over plants.

■ Frequent garage sales and flea markets to look for interesting wooden containers, buckets, or barrels to use for container gardening.

In early spring place mid-size pieces of brush among emerging perennial plants; the brush will serve as natural supports for plants that require staking.

Slender saplings and twine arranged tepee-style make a sturdy trellis for climbing beans. Children will enjoy this shady hideaway, with walls covered with built-in snacks.

Getting the Most from Your Tools

Good tools provide the gardener with steady help. Without the ability to dig deeply with a spade, break up the soil with a fork, or smooth soil with a rake, the gardener works harder. Proper, well-cared-for tools save time, effort, and money in the long run.

Building a Tool Collection

Don't expect a fully stocked garden tool shed the first year. Instead, buy the necessities and add to your collection in future years as you discover what you use and like. Make long-term plans to buy the tools and equipment you need.

When you buy a tool, pick it up, check the balance, and determine how it feels in your hands. Look for solid construction and good-quality materials. Make sure joints are solid, especially at the point where the handle connects to the working end.

Always buy the best quality you can afford. A cheap tool won't last, and you'll spend more in replacements than you would for one good tool.

Purchase sale-priced tools, especially at the end of the gardening season. Expect to find savings of 25 to 50 percent.

The basic ten. Although you may be tempted to buy many interesting tools for specific jobs, you need only a few basic tools. These will serve you well, if you choose them wisely and care for them well.

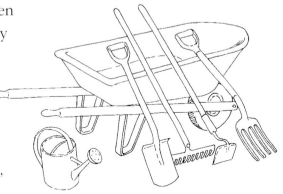

A basic garden tool assortment includes a shovel, rake, hoe, garden fork, wheelbarrow, and watering can.

Spade. Every gardener uses a spade. Choose a sturdy one with good balance and a strong thin blade that won't bend when you dig deep into the soil. Look for a solid shoulder you can step on to increase your push as you dig. Choose one with a D handle for leverage. Some gardeners prefer short handles; others like longer handles. Try different lengths to see which one suits your purpose.

Steel rake. Use a rake to remove loose sticks and rocks and prepare the bed for seeds and plants. A straight handle usually is preferred.

Garden fork. Forks are useful for digging into the soil and breaking up clumps of dirt. Look for well-spaced round or angled prongs with sufficient room between to keep dirt from clogging. Again, a D handle offers more leverage than a straight handle.

Hoe. Use a hoe to lay out rows and loosen soil. They come in different styles, some pointed, some flat; some even swivel.

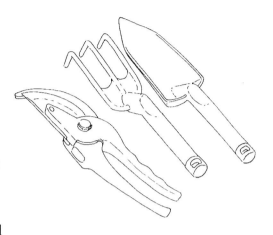

Essential hand tools include a bypass pruner, cultivator, and trowel.

Cultivator. This handy tool helps you break up soil between rows and eliminate weeds.

Watering can. Look for different sizes in either metal or plastic. Plastic cans are cheaper and lighter than metal.

Hand tools. Small trowels or cultivators are helpful when working in beds, planting flowers or vegetables, or loosening soils.

Wheelbarrow. A wheeled cart is useful for moving refuse, soil,

heavy plants, and supplies. Plastic versions are often less expensive and weigh less, which may be preferable to some gardeners.

Pruner. Use a good-quality pruner to shape bushes and remove small limbs from trees.

Sharp garden shears. A big help when cutting blooms or removing faded foliage; shears also cut black plastic and other garden materials.

Tool Care

Keep tools clean. Whether they are new or used, keep them clean. After each use, rub a steel-wool pad over the metal parts to remove dirt. Or, keep a pail of sand mixed with oil where you store your tools. When you finish with a tool, push it in and out of the sand mixture to clean it.

Keep tools in good repair. Never leave your tools outside in bad weather, or lying on the ground for someone to step on or damage.

Check the condition of tools at the end of the season. Tighten screws or fasteners. Examine each tool for nicks, and smooth it with a file. Sharpen cutting edges. It's a waste of time to work with dull tools. When you sharpen, make sure you maintain the shape of the edge. Wipe lightly with oil before storing.

Store tools as close to the garden as possible. You lose valuable time trekking to the basement or garage whenever you need a tool.

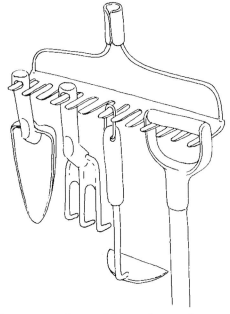

The tines of an old garden rake serve well as hangers for small garden tools.

Build or purchase an inexpensive garden shed to store your tools, pots, fertilizers, baskets, and other supplies in one convenient spot. The simplest version is a shed-type structure built against the side of the house or garage.

Make simple wood hangers for your tools or buy inexpensive plastic hooks. Hang tools together in a garage or shed.

Canvas carpenter's aprons with assorted built-in pockets are available in most hardware departments very inexpensively. These supply easily accessible, portable storage for hand tools, seeds, and other supplies gardeners carry with them. When you finish in the garden, hang the apron with its contents ready for the next time you work. This storage item has an added bonus: it keeps soil off your clothes.

Screw cup hangers around a bushel basket and hang your tools from them. Carry seeds and other needs in the basket.

An old golf cart can be put to work carrying tools around.

A partitioned wooden box or basket, such as an old wine carrier conveniently holds tools you use to work around flowers. All kinds of baskets (often offered at tag sales) make useful containers for the garden.

Place a set of shelves in a garage or shed to store small tools, rags, twine, seed packets, and plant markers. Build one or two shelves of inexpensive wood (recycled from a wooden pallet, for instance).

Paint tool handles bright colors so that you can find them easily if you leave them lying in the garden.

Gardener's Tip

Frequent garage sales in search of sturdy old tools at low prices. Look for well-maintained tools. A little elbow grease and some steel wool shine metal parts. Clean up wooden handles with a light sanding, followed by a coat of oil.

Make Your Own Tools and Equipment

Most gardeners eventually develop a personal method of planting, staking, and separating plants. Some count on special tools they adapt or develop for their unique situation. Custom-made tools can be low- or no-cost items, and often work best.

■ Make your own tools for marking rows or trenches. Take a 4-foot-long piece of scrap wood that is 2 inches wide; mark it off in feet and in 6-inch measures. Use as a guide to space rows and/or plants.

■ Make shallow furrows perfect for planting seeds by wiring a short piece of old picket fence to a rake. Drag the points along the prepared seed bed.

■ Use this old standby to set straight rows: Take two stakes and tie one end of a length of string to each stake. Use as a gauge to mark the distance between rows.

■ Dig in small flower beds with a sturdy cup.

■ Sprinkle fine seeds on a prepared bed with an old salt shaker.

■ Make an inexpensive shelter for transplants. Build a box frame with 2x4s and staple a covering of clear plastic over it. Place it against the south side of a building, if possible. Put your seedlings inside the shelter several weeks before the air is warm enough for them to stand outdoors without protection. (Keep plants well watered.)

■ Install a small stand-alone greenhouse in a sunny spot in your yard. If you build it yourself using recycled materials, it can be inexpensive. Or, look for a greenhouse kit on sale. Even a small greenhouse holds a lot of seedlings. And walking into the moisture-laden, earthy-smelling interior of a greenhouse is a special treat for anyone who loves gardening.

Gardener's Tip

Be sure to leave the top of your cold frame ajar on warm spring days so that the plants do not overheat.

A small cold frame is simple to construct using scrap wood, and its protection allows you to get a good start on the gardening season.

■ Make a simple cold frame from old storm windows. Cold frames are simple frames or shallow boxes, with no top or bottom, sometimes sunk partially into the soil. The unit is usually constructed so the top slopes to the east or southeast in order to collect the most early spring sunlight.

With a cold frame you can start seedlings outside earlier than is possible without protection.

Use sturdy scrap wood for the sides. Build the back higher than the front. Fasten the windows to the back of the frame with hinges, so that you can adjust the opening according to the outside temperature. Make a notched board to serve as a prop that will hold the window open at different angles. Move your plants into the cold frame to harden before you plant them in the garden. Or start seedlings directly in the cold frame a bit earlier than you can plant them outdoors. Water plants in the cold frame regularly.

Gardening for Your Home

Vegetables and herbs from your own garden taste better than store-bought and save grocery money as well. If you preserve some for year-round use, you'll save even more.

Gourmet Gardens

If you set aside an area to grow a few vegetables, the savings really mount. You'll be surprised how easy it is to grow even specialty vegetables that command premium prices in stores. As with flower gardening, you can save even more by eliminating the cost of nursery-grown seedlings and starting your own seeds indoors in early spring.

■ Grow tiny luxury salad greens, such as radicchio or zippy arugula, which add piquancy and color to salads.

■ Try offbeat varieties of vegetables such as purple beans, yellow peppers, or exotic Asian vegetables that add authenticity to your stir-fries.

■ If eggplant suits your fancy, try the prolific miniature varieties supermarkets sell at high prices.

Gardener's Tip

Extend your season by making several small plantings of beans, lettuces, and other fast-growing crops a week or two apart.

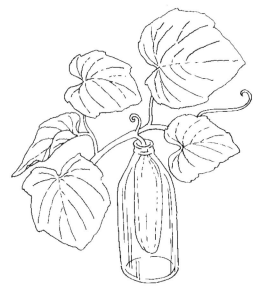

Children will enjoy the mystery of how the fat cucumber got into the small-mouthed jar. Slip the jar over the immature fruit and let the cuke develop inside the jar.

■ Even in season, corn is never cheap. With corn in your garden, you can pick and eat it before the sugar disappears, and never mind the cost.

■ Experience the luxury of having all the leeks you can possibly use in soups or stews for the cost of a packet of seeds.

■ If pickles are a family favorite, save money by growing cucumbers. Make delicious pickles at a fraction of the cost of store-bought ones.

These rows of cabbage, beans, and squash are well mulched with shredded leaves.

Easy recipes take the work out of preparation. You don't even have to process some kinds, half sours for instance.

■ Start an asparagus bed. You'll have access to one of the most delicious and most expensive products in the food basket. Once you establish an asparagus bed, expect to pick for 20 years without a care about the cost.

■ Perennial rhubarb and horseradish also come back every year with little or no care.

Gardener's Tip

In some areas, you may be able to sell your excess produce at a small stand in front of your house or at a local farmers' market. Make your garden pay for itself.

Herb Gardens

Culinary herbs have gained popularity in recent years.

■ If you grow a few basil plants you'll have enough leaves to make all the pesto you want. Freeze some for winter pasta treats.

■ Grow both curly and Italian parsley for variety in the garden and in your cooking.

■ Mint plants grow so easily they tend to take over the herb garden.

■ Thyme makes a lovely ground cover and adds flavor to many different dishes.

■ The taste of fresh oregano is light years away from dried.

■ Plant dill once — it reseeds itself and you'll have an abundance year after year.

■ Shallots and garlic are two vegetables good cooks can't live without. Grow your own; they keep well in a cool place. After an initial investment you need never buy any more. Just hold back some of the cloves to plant next year. When the leaves brown and collapse, allow them to dry completely, then store them in a cool place.

Gardener's Tip

Make an inexpensive drying rack with pegs to hold bunches of herbs. Or spread them on old screens stacked with blocks of wood between.

Give herbs plenty of sun in an accessible spot near the kitchen, if possible. Start plants from seed or buy a few plants. If you know other herb gardeners, chances are they'll pot up some to share. Dry herbs for winter use in bouquets, wreaths, and sachets, as well as in recipes.

Gardener's Tip

Use a fragrant mixture of your dried herbs to fill tiny calico bags for a special sachet.

This small herb garden is bordered on the left with garlic chives and on the right with santolina; in the foreground are oregano, 'Lemon Gem' marigold, and johnny-jump-ups; behind are thymes, chives, nasturtiums, violas, and purple basil.

Drying Flowers and Herbs

If you have ever priced dried arrangements or wreaths, you know they are costly. Drying techniques are easy to master. If you grow and dry your own material, however, you eliminate most of the expense of producing these popular decorations.

You can collect a wealth of plant material for dried arrangements growing naturally and freely along roadsides and in fields. To add special colors and textures, however, grow your own selection of plants suited to drying.

Statice, strawflowers, and other everlastings dry well, and they are easy and inexpensive to start from seed. All are lovely in wreaths and other dried arrangements.

Pick your materials on a dry, sunny morning. Harvest just before plants reach their prime. As they dry, they continue to mature. If you wait until flowers fully open before picking, the dried material will look tired.

Tie the stems together with string, then hang in a warm, airy place, near an oil burner, for instance, or in a warm, dry attic.

■ Statice comes in mixed shades of subtle colors and in bolder individual tones. It needs full sun and well-drained soil. Sow inside six to eight weeks before planting outdoors.

■ Starflowers with their stiff stems fit nicely into dried arrangements. Their heads, once dried, turn a light brown with tiny florets, each with a starlike center.

■ Strawflowers grow on compact stems in every color except blue.

■ Baby's-breath grows easily and sports an abundance of tiny pink or white flowers all summer long. It dries beautifully, adding a delicate note to arrangements.

To dry herbs and flowers like these Chinese-lantern plants, globe amaranth, and statice, tie stems together with string, and hang in a warm, airy place.

Preserving the Harvest

Want to feel really frugal? Preserve as much as possible of the harvest. Your savings mount when you store some of your bounty in a freezer, cold cellar, or pantry shelf. With your produce safely stored, you will eat well for months after the harvest and continue to save on grocery bills.

If you dry fruits and vegetables, you won't even have the costs of running a freezer or processing for canning. Plant varieties that have been developed for the storage method you plan to use.

Cucumbers. Pickle excess cucumbers or plant some just for that purpose. Half-sours take little more than packing in a crock or large jar, then adding a simple pickling solution. Or, cut cukes whenever you have enough for a batch of bread-and-butter pickles, and process.

Tomatoes. Canning tomatoes takes more work, but when you eat them you know they are cheap and pure, without preservatives.

To avoid the chore of canning, wash tomatoes, remove the stem ends, turn them upside down into freezer bags, and freeze. When you need tomatoes for a sauce or soup, run each one quickly under warm water — voilá, the skin slips off like a charm. Add a sprig of parsley and/or basil to each bag for instant herb seasoning.

Dried tomatoes are currently very popular and pricey. But you can dry your own. Dip tomatoes in boiling water, then slip off skins. Remove cores. Cut into ⅛-inch slices or ¼-inch cubes. Spread in a single layer on a tray.

■ To dry in hot sun, provide good air circulation. When the tops are dry, turn the tomatoes and dry the other side. This method takes one to two days in good weather.

■ To dry tomatoes in an oven, place the tray in a 120°F oven for 18 to 24 hours. Turn once or twice, and rotate trays.

Store dried tomatoes in clean jars in the refrigerator. Refresh by placing them on a shallow plate and spraying with warm water;

let them soften for about an hour.

Winter squash and onions. Dry these well; they keep for months in a cool, dry place.

Green peppers freeze beautifully without any blanching. Cut into sizes you prefer for a handy recipe-ready vegetable. Or leave whole for stuffing. Seal in plastic bags.

Flavored vinegars. Making gourmet vinegars offers a perfect way to prolong the herb harvest. Wash freshly picked sprigs of herbs. Place about 1 cup of herbs in 2 cups of apple cider, wine, or other vinegar. Add some balsamic vinegar, if you choose. Bottle and allow to steep for two to three weeks until flavor develops. Strain into clean, sterilized bottles.

For fruit vinegars, use 1 pound of soft summer fruit such as raspberries, blueberries, or peaches. Place in a sterilized jar. Add 5 cups of white wine vinegar. Seal with an airtight cover. Steep

Among the many satisfying results of a home garden are the fruits of the harvest.

for a week or two. Strain the mixture into a saucepan, pressing the fruit to extract the juice and flavor. Add 1 teaspoon sugar and simmer over very low heat for about 10 minutes. Fill sterilized jars with the vinegar, adding a few fresh berries for visual appeal. Then visit a gourmet store to see how much you saved!

Index